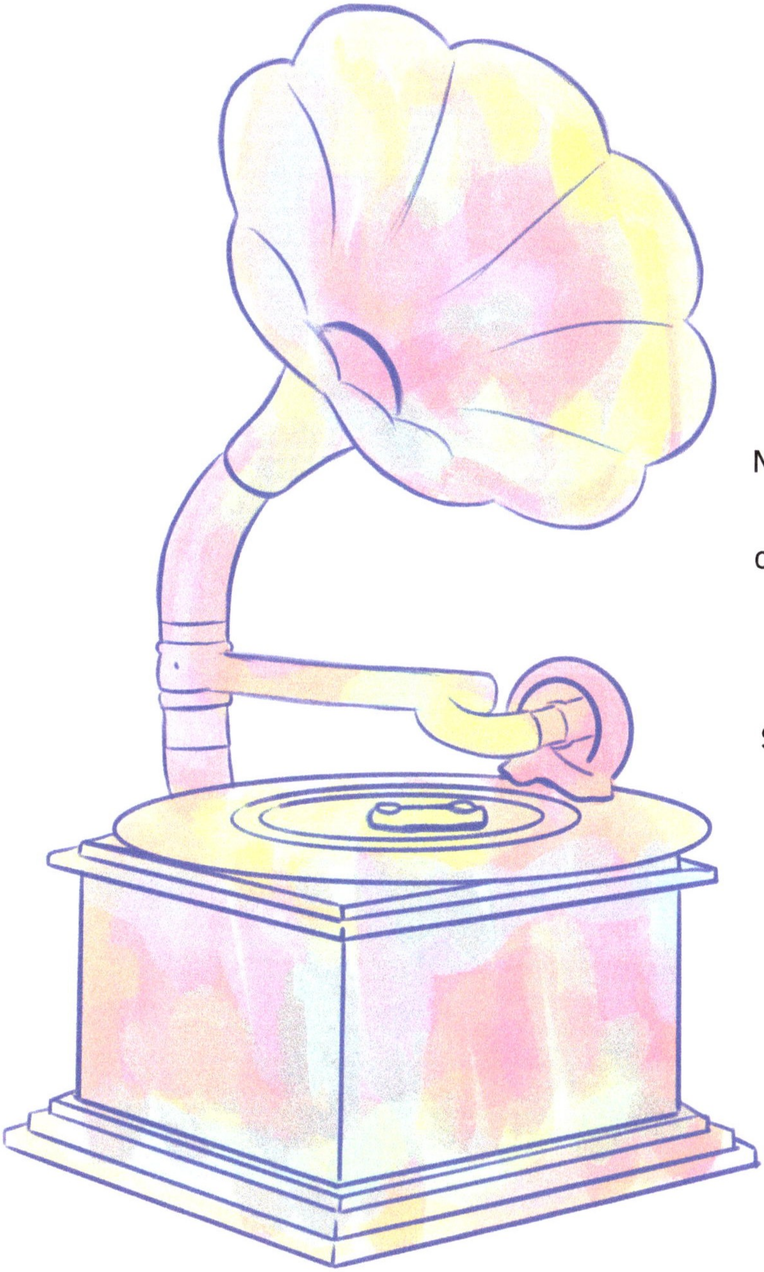

No portion of this book may be reproduced in any form without permission from the publisher, except as permitted by U.S. copyright law. For permissions contact the author.

All rights reserved.

Copyright © 2022 Flisadam Pointer

Sweet Sounds: The ABCs of Black Women in Music by Flisadam Pointer

Published in the United States by Pointer Publishing LLC, PO Box 5115, Hillside, New Jersey 07205.

www.pointerpublishing.com

ISBN 978-1-7377422-0-3
Ebook ISBN 978-1-7377422-1-0

Cover designed by and illustrations by Ameerah Singh.

Printed in United States of America.

First Edition

To my munchkins.

May music be your faithful guide throughout life. I hope this book fuels that journey.

Sweet Sounds

THE ABCs OF BLACK WOMEN IN MUSIC

WRITTEN BY FLISADAM POINTER ILLUSTRATED BY AMEERAH SINGH

Aa

Aretha Franklin

When **a**ddressing **A**retha you better **a**dd **a** miss in front of her name because this **a**ngelic vocalist is **a**ll about her *R-E-S-P-E-C-T!*

Birthdate March 25, 1942 | Hometown Detroit, MI, USA

Billie Holiday

Ain't Nobody's Business how Billie sings those beautiful ballads about the broken-hearted blues.

Birthdate April 17, 1915 | Hometown Baltimore, MD, USA

Cc

Chaka Khan

After **C**haka and her **c**rimson **c**oils take **c**enter stage her ability to **c**arry a tune is always sweet *Like Sugar.*

Birthdate March 23, 1953 | Hometown Chicago, IL, USA

Dd

Dionne Warwick

Dionne is not *Daydreaming* when she **d**elightfully **d**eclares herself the **d**azzling grande **d**ame all of entertainment.

Birthdate December 12, 1940 | Hometown Orange, NJ, USA

Ee

Ella Fitzgerald

Whether you are *Cheek To Cheek* or just within **e**arshot of **E**lla as she is **e**ntertaining, **e**veryone **e**xplodes with **e**motion after **e**ach **e**vangelical note.

Birthdate April 25, 1917 | Hometown Harlem, NY, USA

Florence Mills

This **f**earless **f**iery performer takes **f**light anytime she is on stage. This is why **F**lorence is **f**amously called *Blackbird.*

Birthdate January 25, 1896 | Hometown Washington, DC, USA

Gladys Knight

Giant groups gleefully gather to groove out on Gladys' *Midnight Train to Georgia.*

Birthdate May 28, 1944 | Hometown Atlanta, GA, USA

Heather Headley

Heather isn't always **h**umming to **h**eartfelt **h**armonies. She **h**as **h**obbies to **h**elp **h**er practice *Me Time*.

Birthdate October 5, 1974 | Hometown Barataria, San Juan, Trinidad and Tobago

Ii

Irene Cara

What A Feeling **i**t **i**s to watch **I**rene **i**nk the **i**ncredible **i**deas from her **i**magination **i**nto a song.

Birthdate March 18, 1959 | Hometown Bronx, NY, USA

Jj

Jennifer Holliday

And I'm Telling You the way Jennifer jovially jolts out notes any jealousy from others is justifiable.

Birthdate October 19, 1960 | Hometown Houston, TX, USA

Kim Weston

It Takes Two, good **k**arma, and a **k**azoo to **k**eep up with the **k**nocking vocal notes of **K**im. Even she **k**nows this.

Birthdate December 20, 1939 | Hometown Detroit, MI, USA

LaVern Baker

For a long time, LaVern has lured listeners in with her light lyrics and lively love songs like *Tra La La*.

Birthdate November 11, 1929 | Hometown Chicago, IL, USA

Ma Rainey

Those moody *Moonshine Blues* were made memorable by Ma, the mother of modern music.

Birthdate April 26, 1886 | Hometown Columbus, GA, USA

Nn

Nina Simone

Call it **n**aivete, but there's **n**o place in this **n**ation where the **n**ostalgic **n**otes of **N**ina won't leave you *Feeling Good*.

Birthdate February 21, 1933 | Hometown Troy, NC, USA

Odetta

Glory Glory to out of this world musician and outspoken activist, Odetta, who took an oath to help others fight oppression.

Birthdate December 31, 1930 | Hometown Birmingham, AL, USA

Patti LaBelle

No matter the place, a palace, or a packed playground, Patti's powerful performance will send you *Over The Rainbow*.

Birthdate May 24, 1944 | Hometown Philadelphia, PA, USA

Queen Latifah

After a few *Quiet Nights Of Quiet Stars* and quippy quotables from Queen any questions about her quaint talents will be quashed.

Birthdate March 18, 1970 | Hometown Newark, NJ, USA

Roberta Flack

Roberta has a relaxing romantic register and resounding range that reminds us *To Love Somebody.*

Birthdate February 10, 1937 | Hometown Arlington, VA, USA

Sarah Vaughan

The **s**ultry **s**ongs **S**arah **s**ings on **s**tage are **s**imilar to *Stardust* because it leaves others feeling **s**hiny and **s**pecial.

Birthdate March 27, 1924 | Hometown Newark, NJ, USA

Tina Turner

The **t**imeless **t**unes of **T**ina should be **t**aught in a class because she is simply *The Best*.

Birthdate November 26, 1939 | Hometown Nutbush, TN, USA

Uu

Ultra Naté

Ultra is **u**ndeniably **u**nique in all of the efforts she **u**ses to **u**nlock her **u**ltimate *Turn It Up* grooves.

Birthdate March 20, 1968 | Hometown Baltimore, MD, USA

Victoria Spivey

If **V**ictoria could have gone **v**iral for her *Funny Feather* she would have or at the **v**ery least her **v**ibrant **v**ibrato.

Birthdate October 15, 1906 | Hometown Houston, TX, USA

Whitney Houston

When *You Believe*, **w**ish, and **w**ork hard for **w**hat you **w**ant like **W**hitney did for her music you **w**ill **w**itness **w**onders.

Birthdate August 9, 1963 | Hometown Newark, NJ, USA

Xênia França

After e**x**periencing the e**x**traordinaire mi**x** **X**ênia offers in her music you will feel like you can *Reach The Stars* in any gala**x**y.

Birthdate February 27, 1986 | Hometown Candeias, Bahia, Brazil

Yvonne Chaka Chaka

Yvonne and her youthful yodel will make you yearn to visit the *Motherland*.

Birthdate May 18, 1982 | Hometown Dobsonville, Soweto, South Africa

Zola Taylor

Zealous when **z**eroed into her *Enchanted* **z**one, **Z**ola can vocally **z**igzag with the best of them.

Birthdate March 17, 1938 | Hometown Los Angeles, CA, USA

www.ingramcontent.com/pod-product-compliance
Lightning Source LLC
Chambersburg PA
CBHW061121170426
43209CB00013B/1630